WARRIOR

GUTS AND GLORY

by Catherine Chambers
Illustrated by Jason Juta

HUNGRY
TOMATO™

CONTENTS

Introducing Military Leaders

What makes a military leader?

Some military leaders were the sons or daughters of kings and queens (such as Alexander the Great, right, the son of King Phillip II of Macedonia), or of generals or famous warriors. They felt it was their duty to carry on wars begun by their parents. Some decided to do even better and further expand their territory. Most of these leaders were educated from a young age in the art of warfare, weaponry, tactics and the politics of their region.

Other military leaders seemed to spring up from nowhere. They were driven by a strong determination to defend or free their people. These leaders often became more ambitious, and went on to increase their power and influence.

Alexander the Great
356–323 BCE

Genghis Khan
1162–1227

Vlad III 1431–1477

Lozen
1840s–1890

Hannibal
247–181 BCE

Oda Nobunaga
1534–1582

Khotol Tsagaan
1260–1306

Toussaint Louverture
1743–1803

Queen Amina
of Zaria
about 1500s

Saladin
1137–1193

Great Military Leaders of the World

WHY GO TO WAR?

Some military leaders went to war to gain territory. This gave them more resources and control of new trade routes, making them wealthier. Others launched attacks to defend their territory and trade routes against aggressive neighbours. Some campaigned to defend their faith, others to expand their faith's influence. All these leaders used horrific methods to reach their goals.

Most of their gains did not last into modern times. But the impact of their conquests can be felt to this day, and they changed the course of history. For these mighty military leaders spread cultures and financial and political systems that we still recognize in the places that they conquered.

In this book, modern place names are given on the maps to show where in the world these warrior leaders lived and fought.

WHAT DID GREAT MILITARY LEADERS SAY?

Leaders did not have much time to write their diaries, but they are thought to have said some bold things.

Alexander the Great: 'I am not afraid of an army of lions led by a sheep. I am afraid of an army of sheep led by a lion.'

Hannibal: 'We will either find a way, or make one.'

Genghis Khan: 'If you are afraid, don't do it. If you are doing it, don't be afraid.'

Genghis Khan

GREAT BATTLES

At the Battle of Issus in 333BCE, Alexander charged straight through enemy lines at King Darius of Persia. Losing his nerve, Darius fled in his chariot, with his enormous army following behind.

TOP TACTICS

Alexander began an assault with an angled central column of foot soldiers, called *pezhetairoi*. He then led a cavalry charge on the right. A trusted general led another charge on the left.

TRUTH OR LEGEND?

In his lifetime, Alexander was seen as a god, the son of Zeus. Later, some said that he was the son of an Egyptian wizard-king; others, that in India he met Amazons, enormous women warriors.

FEROCIOUS FACTS

● Alexander's army looted, plundered and killed children.

● His influence spread over 5 million sq km (2 million sq miles).

● Some scientists say that Alexander was murdered by poisoning.

Macedonia
Black Sea
Caspian Sea
Turkmenistan
Battle of Hydaspes
Battle of Issus
ALEXANDER THE GREAT'S EMPIRE
Mediterranean Sea
Pakistan
Iran
Egypt
Saudi Arabia
→ = war route
Arabian Sea

ALEXANDER THE GREAT

Alexander of Macedonia led a terrifying army across ancient Greek states and east as far as India. His father, Philip, had left him a highly disciplined force, trained to use the 18-ft (5.5-m) sarissa. This spear was the longest used by any army, and it allowed Alexander's men to attack first. He always led his cavalry from the front, astride his beloved horse, Bucephalus. His infantry moved in a phalanx, a formation of tight rows. Alexander saw his enemy clearly and reacted quickly to their mistakes, while his daring inspired his own army to fight even harder.

WHERE
Kingdom of Macedonia – lands around the north-west Aegean Sea

WHEN
356–323BCE

HANNIBAL

Hannibal was a great North African general who used brilliant tactics to recapture lands from the Romans in the Second Punic War – though his own forces were very much smaller. He used all means of transport, including 37 elephants, to cross the Pyrenees and Alps into the Roman heartland, Italy. Even here, Hannibal defeated the Romans, always using the terrain to his advantage. He forced them into valleys, stringing out their troops in lines that were hard to defend. He squeezed them against mountains and closed off access to food and water.

HANNIBAL'S MARCH TO ITALY

France

Pyrenees

Alps

Battle of Trasimene

Spain

Italy

Rome

Mediterranean Sea

AFRICA   Carthage

GREAT BATTLES

At the Battle of Trasimene (217BCE), Hannibal hid his troops in a fog over Lake Trasimene. Roman troops moved towards them and Hannibal's army drove thousands of them into the lake.

TOP TACTICS

Hannibal knew when his enemy was following him and at dusk led them into difficult positions. Then at night he placed his troops around the enemy and ambushed them in daylight.

TRUTH OR LEGEND?

Hannibal's deadly deeds were written by Romans! Did they portray him as superhuman to make his final defeat seem even greater? The origin of his elephants puzzles historians to this day.

FEROCIOUS FACTS

• In the Alps, Hannibal's engineers used fire and vinegar to break up huge rocks blocking their way.

• Hannibal's troops killed up to 70,000 Romans at the Battle of Cannae (216BCE), his greatest victory.

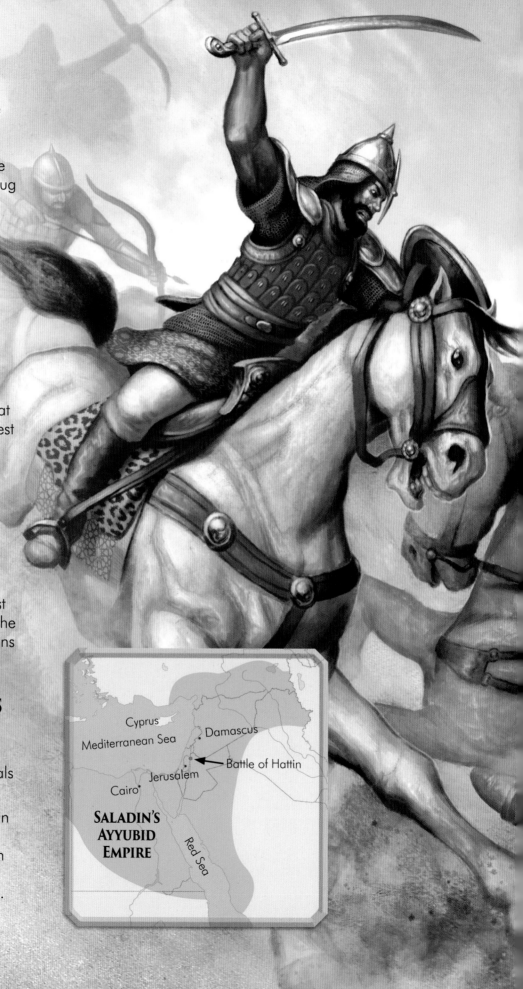

GREAT BATTLES

On 2 October 1187, Saladin finally ousted the Christian Franks from Jerusalem. He attacked the city walls with massive catapults. Saladin then dug down below one section, making it collapse.

TOP TACTICS

Saladin united the Arab commanders of small armies that were always fighting each other. He rallied them to fight for a common cause. Then he carefully chose battles that gave his cause the greatest advantage.

TRUTH OR LEGEND?

In legend, Saladin was honourable towards his enemy. He even offered gifts to one of his greatest foes, England's Richard the Lionheart. So far, historians say that all this is true.

FEROCIOUS FACTS

● Saladin terrified his enemy with gongs, trumpets, clashing cymbals and yelling men.

● At the Battle of Hattin in 1187, Saladin executed most of the elite Christian military: the Knights Templar and Hospitallers.

Cyprus

Mediterranean Sea

Damascus

Battle of Hattin

Jerusalem

Cairo

SALADIN'S AYYUBID EMPIRE

Red Sea

SALADIN

Through stunning military skill, Saladin united Egypt, much of Syria, Yemen and northern Iraq under his Ayyubid dynasty. He then tackled the Christian Crusaders who were competing with Muslims to rule the Holy Land, especially Jerusalem. Tactically, Saladin launched lightning strikes on the enemy's front and rear. His elite cavalries from Arab and Turkish or Bedouin and Nubian forces ram-raided and scattered the foe, firing arrows and javelins. They isolated enemy units, then surrounded and killed them with their short swords. The rest of the cavalry thundered in behind.

WHERE
Mesopotamia, now Iraq

WHEN
about 1137–1193

GENGHIS KHAN

WHERE
Mongolia

WHEN
1162–1227

Genghis Khan created the vast Mongol Empire by first uniting nomadic tribes on Asia's grassland steppes. He then moved with his swift cavalry to gain territory, from China in the east to Europe's Adriatic Sea in the west. Genghis Khan travelled with technical advisers and engineers. In his movable ger (below), they spent months mapping the terrain he would cover. A favourite battle tactic was the false retreat, turning back suddenly on the enemy. Genghis Khan bombarded cities mercilessly, and trampled and burned all before him so that the enemy could not rise again.

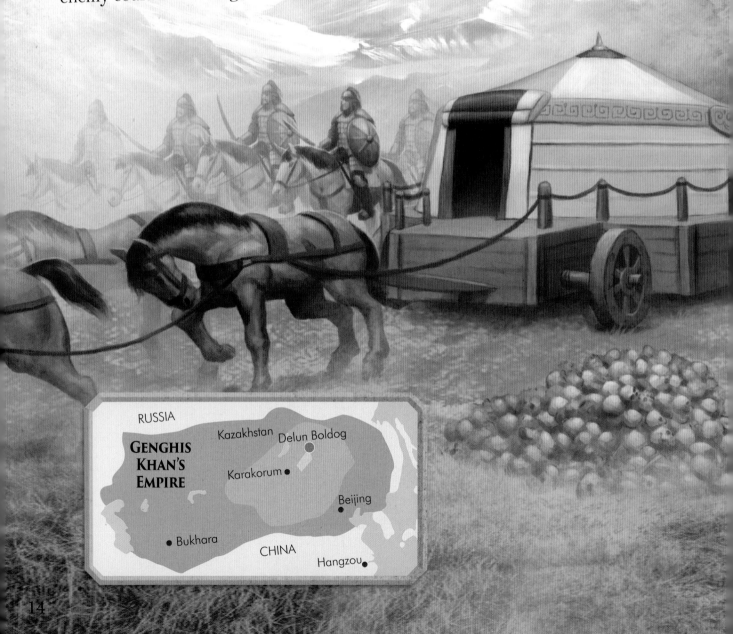

GENGHIS KHAN'S EMPIRE

RUSSIA

Kazakhstan Delun Boldog

Karakorum •

Beijing •

• Bukhara

CHINA

Hangzou •

GREAT BATTLES

In the war against the great Persian Khwarezmid Empire (1218–20), Genghis Khan sent in spies to threaten its citizens and divide its army. Then the slaughter began.

TOP TACTICS

Genghis Khan was a master of deception. He saddled straw soldiers on spare horses to make his cavalry seem larger. He lit many campfires to give the impression of a vast army.

TRUTH OR LEGENDS

In legend, Genghis Khan was born with a blood clot in his hand. His ancestor was a grey wolf! Some say these were signs of greatness; others, that they showed a ruthless genius.

FEROCIOUS FACTS

● Genghis Khan slaughtered friendly Mongolian nomad leaders, taking over their armies.

● He murdered any defeated Tatar (from an ancient Asiatic tribe) who was taller than the axle of a cartwheel, leaving hordes of orphaned children.

GREAT BATTLES

Khutulun used spies, smokescreens, false retreats, ambush and lightning attacks against Kublai Khan. But she only managed to help her father to hold his own territory.

TOP TACTICS

Khutulun advised her father on which enemy to attack. Many Mongol rulers, including the great Genghis Khan, valued the tactical opinions of women.

TRUTH OR LEGEND?

Khutulun vowed to marry any man who could beat her at wrestling. Each man who lost had to give her 100 horses. Khutulun ended up with 10,000 horses!

FEROCIOUS FACTS

● Khutulun would leave her father's side, dash into the enemy and return with a foe, dead or alive.

● She could even fight while riding her horse backwards. Her 14 older brothers could not match her skills.

KHOTOL TSAGAAN

A descendant of Genghis Khan, Khotol Tsagaan was the daughter of Kaidu, ruler of Mongolia and Turkestan. She was also known as Khutulun, and took part in her father's later fierce battles against his brother, Kublai Khan of China. Khutulun's smart battle tactics, psychological warfare and political knowledge of the region made her essential to her father's campaigns. Her riding and archery skills were second to none. A famous Italian travel writer, Marco Polo, described Khutulun as big and strong. She could snatch an enemy as easily as a hawk snatches a bird.

WHERE
Turkestan and Mongolia

WHEN
about 1260–1306

VLAD III

WHERE
Principality of
Wallachia in present-
day Romania

WHEN
1431–about 1477

Vlad III fought savagely to regain and retain Wallachia, once ruled by his father. At times he made enemies of nearby Hungarians or powerful Ottoman Turks. At others, he cunningly sought each as allies. This terrifying prince was also known as Vlad Dracula, Vlad Tepes and Vlad the Impaler. His tactic of impaling the enemy on rows of sharpened sticks gave him the last two names. Vlad organized his small army well, using ambush, night attacks, sabotage and other guerrilla tactics.

VLAD III'S
WALLACHIA,
NOW IN MODERN
ROMANIA

EUROPE Hungary

Romania

Ottoman Turkish
Empire

Transylvania

Wallachia

GREAT BATTLES

Vlad tried to push the Ottomans towards the River Danube. But the Ottoman army was three times greater than his own. Still, he impaled 20,000 enemy troops and freed Wallachia, for a while.

TOP TACTICS

Vlad often invited rivals to feast at his court. Then he murdered them. He first used this tactic on nobles whom he suspected of betraying his father to Hungarian troops.

TRUTH OR LEGEND?

Folk tales relate that Vlad executed between 40,000 and 100,000 captives. The numbers may not be true, but he probably did publicly torture, maim and execute many.

FEROCIOUS FACTS

- Vlad severed his enemies' arms, legs and noses.

- He left his maimed captives out in the cold to be devoured by wolves.

GREAT BATTLES

Queen Amina swept southwards for hundreds of miles, crushing and controlling greater kingdoms, such as Nupe and Jukun. Her greatest assets were her swift horses, imported at great expense from lands north of the Sahara.

TOP TACTICS

Queen Amina surrounded her military camps with protective ditches and high, gated walls. She defended Zaria city in this way, too. The walls can be seen to this day.

TRUTH OR LEGEND?

Was Queen Amina born a warrior? Legend tells that she loved fighting, even as a small child. It is said that as a toddler her grandmother caught her clutching a dagger.

FEROCIOUS FACTS

● Amina's used her cutlass skilfully to slash the iron helmets and mail of her more powerful rivals.

● It is said that she picked a captured soldier every night and murdered him.

QUEEN AMINA OF ZARIA

With her superb tactics, Queen Amina increased the power
and wealth of Zaria, a city kingdom of the Hausa people.
From the age of 16, she led her cavalry across West Africa's
Sahel grasslands. Horses were rare in this area and gave
Amina a great military advantage. For 34 years she subdued
other, greater Hausa kingdoms. Her influence extended over
3,200 km (2,000 miles) westwards to the Atlantic Ocean. She
forced all defeated powers to pay to continue trading across the Sahara. This trade
in salt, gold, potash, leather goods, livestock and slaves led to Zaria's greatness.

WHERE
Zazzau, now Zaria,
northern Nigeria

WHEN
about 1500s

WEST AFRICA

Atlantic
Ocean

Algeria

THE SAHARA

Libya

Mali

Niger

Chad

**QUEEN AMINA
CONTROLLED TRADE
ROUTES SOUTH OF
THE SAHARA**

Zaria

Nigeria

Major overland trade routes in the 1500s

ODA NOBUNAGA

WHERE
Owari, Japan

WHEN
1534–1582

Nobunaga was determined to be more powerful than his minor warlord father and ended up uniting half the feudal states of Japan. Nobunaga defeated far stronger armies than his own, using ambush, daring attacks and a new weapon, the musket, imported from Europe. With these muskets, savage swords, spears and his tight, disciplined units, Nobunaga first united Owari province. Then he tackled other provinces until he reached the capital, Kyoto, securing the vital seaport of Osaka. Nobunaga established a strong economy in every territory that he gained. This gave him the wealth to continue his battles.

ODA NOBUNAGA'S EMPIRE

East Japan

Central Japan

Battle of Okehazama

Kyoto

Osaka

West Japan

GREAT BATTLES

At the Battle of Okehazama in 1560, Nobunaga's 3,000 troops faced 25,000 commanded by the great Imagawa Yoshimoto. With stealth and aided by a distracting thunderstorm, Nobunaga ambushed them in a gorge.

TOP TACTICS

Nobunaga used deceit and decoys to confuse and trap his enemy in difficult terrain. He made dummy soldiers from straw, topped with helmets. Then he set flags among them.

TRUTH OR LEGEND?

Some say Nobunaga was a demon king because he ruthlessly burned people alive. Others say that he was seen as evil only after his death. Nobunaga saw himself as a living god.

FEROCIOUS FACTS

● Nobunaga ruthlessly burned Buddhist monasteries outside Kyoto and slaughtered the powerful warrior monks.

● In 1574 he set fire to an enemy fortress at Nagashima, massacring 20,000 men, women and children inside.

GREAT BATTLES

Toussaint first fought alongside the British to rid St Domingue of its French rulers. But the British later became his enemy and in 1800 Toussaint defeated them in seven battles over seven days.

TOP TACTICS

Toussaint spread his units out over thick forest. There, he waited patiently for the enemy. He then drew his units in around his foe, surrounding and finally attacking them.

TRUTH OR LEGEND?

In legend, Toussaint's father was Gaou-Ginou, a chieftain from the Arada people of West Africa. This tale gave him high status – but in reality his father was probably an educated slave called Pierre Baptiste Simon.

FEROCIOUS FACTS

● Toussaint's troops burned sugar plantations and murdered hated slave owners. Toussaint saved the less brutal owners.

● Farming tool weapons included vicious cane-cutting machete knives.

● Toussaint killed Spanish churchgoers who were attending Mass.

Atlantic Ocean

Caribbean Sea

Cuba

Jamaica

Hispaniola Island

Haiti

Dominican Replublic

Puerto Rico

TOUSSAINT LOUVERTURE'S CARIBBEAN

TOUSSAINT LOUVERTURE

Toussaint Louverture was the inspiring leader of the only successful slave revolt in the Americas. Toussaint was a freed slave on St Domingue, a French colony on the west side of the island of Hispaniola. In 1791 he joined freedom fighters to rid St Domingue of its brutal sugar plantation slave owners, and the French. Toussaint used stealth to spot gaps in his enemy's defence, and the terrain to stalk and ambush his foe. His first weapons were farming tools, cutlasses and pointed sticks. After freeing St Domingue, Toussaint defeated invading British troops and the Spanish rulers of Hispaniola's east side.

WHERE
St Domingue, now Haiti, on Hispaniola Island, Caribbean

WHEN
1743–1803

LOZEN

WHERE
Chiricahua Apache
homelands, USA

WHEN
Late 1840s–1890

Lozen fought with guile and strength to defend her people, the Chiricahua Apache, against the United States, who had taken their lands. She joined her brother Victorio's band to strike at both US and Mexican troops. Lozen located them from far away, waiting in high crags overlooking trails. Using her knowledge of the landscape, she then surrounded and ambushed them. Lozen could train any horse and ride it up rocky mountains and across raging rivers. She was lethal with a rifle and a knife. Yet, despite her great warrior's skills, Lozen could not free her people.

SOUTH-WESTERN UNITED STATES

Colorado River

Rio Grande

Arizona

CHIRICAHUA APACHE HOMELANDS

New Mexico

Gila River

Mexico

GREAT BATTLES

After Victorio's death, Lozen joined Geronimo, the famous Apache warrior. In one battle, he ran out of ammunition. So Lozen crawled towards enemy fire and stole a stash of bullets.

TOP TACTICS

Lozen built decoy camps to trick the enemy. Her superb survival skills meant that she knew when her foe was weakened by lack of food and water.

TRUTH OR LEGEND?

In legend, young Lozen climbed the Sacred Salinas Mountain to receive special powers from the spirits. She returned with a mystical sense that helped her locate the Chiricahua Apache's enemies.

FEROCIOUS FACTS

● Victorio said, 'Lozen is my right hand...strong as a man, braver than most, and cunning in strategy.'

● In 1879, Victorio's band killed eight people in US Captain Ambrose's camp, stealing 46 horses.

Famous Battles

Alexander the Great and the Battle of Hydaspes River (326bce)

Alexander had swept through Greece, Egypt, the Middle East and Persia. Now it was time to tackle India and beyond. His main obstacle was King Porus, who held an area now in Pakistan's Panjab region. Alexander surprised his foe by crossing the River Jhelum in full monsoon flood to face him. King Porus commanded a mighty army of infantry, cavalry and towering elephants. It was three times larger than Alexander's force but Alexander's tactics were superior. His cavalry launched a storm of arrows that attacked Porus's left side, while his pikemen pushed back the elephants. Finally, Alexander used his other generals to attack the enemy's rear and surround King Porus's army.

Hannibal and the Battle of Cannae (216bce)

Hannibal and his army had crossed the Pyrenees Mountains and the towering Alps, defeating bands of fierce-fighting tribes all the way. Now, he faced the Romans at the village of Cannae. About 80,000 Roman troops advanced confidently, the sea behind them and the River Aufidus to their right. They pushed forward with most of their troops in a long line, thinking that this would relentlessly crush Hannibal's 50,000 soldiers. Hannibal deployed his Gallic and Spanish troops in the centre, Africans at their sides and cavalry on their wings, in a crescent shape. As the Romans moved forward, Hannibal's crescent encircled and trapped them, defeating them heavily.

SALADIN AND THE BATTLE OF HATTIN (1187)

Saladin had made a truce with the Christian Crusader states. It was broken, though, by Reginald of Chatillon. This French Crusader had attacked Muslim trading caravans crossing the Holy Land. It was now all-out war. Saladin attacked the city of Tiberias on the west side of the Sea of Galilee. The Crusaders were camped about 32 km (20 miles) from Galilee and decided to march towards their enemy. But they grew weak from thirst and Saladin's cavalry strikes. Saladin used this advantage to pin the Crusaders back to two great hills, the Horns of Hattin. The Crusaders were slaughtered and Saladin himself took the life of Reginald of Chatillon.

GENGHIS KHAN'S XIXIA CAMPAIGN, CHINA (1205–1210)

Genghis Khan wanted to attack the great Jin Empire to the north of the Yangtze River. But he knew that he must first defeat the north-western state of Xixia. If he did not, the Xixia might hit his flank as he drove towards Jin. So, after a few quick assaults to unsettle the Xixia, he launched a full invasion. In 1209 Genghis and his troops trekked across the Gobi Desert, clouting the Xixia's Wolohai fortress. He then led his cavalry over high mountains to the capital, Yinchuan. Here he made a false retreat, drawing out Xixia troops and capturing their commander. Yinchuan surrendered after Genghis flooded it with water – which rushed down and flooded his troops!

VLAD III'S NIGHT ATTACK (17 JUNE 1462)

Vlad III had impaled thousands of Turks, angering Mehmet II, ruler of Turkey. So Vlad was faced with Mehmet's 300,000 troops, which vastly outnumbered his own. At the River Danube, Vlad met Mehmet's army in a brief clash. He then retreated to Targoviste, Wallachia's capital. As he marched, Vlad poisoned wells and burned food stores to starve Mehmet's oncoming troops. He also ordered stealth attacks on them. Then, at dead of night on 17 June, Vlad launched an all-out attack on Mehmet's camp, slaughtering thousands.

MORE FEROCIOUS FACTS

- Alexander the Great let nothing get in his way. He completely wiped out a top Greek enemy unit called the Sacred Band of Thebes. At Persepolis, he burned down a Persian palace in revenge for a defeat 100 years earlier!

- Lozen fought more battles for the Chiricahua Apache than any other fighter, including the great Geronimo and even her brother Victorio. She would locate the enemy by praying alone in the desert. She kept turning around until she felt a trembling sensation in her hands, which indicated the direction and strength of her foe.

- To this day, Queen Amina of Zaria is called 'Amina, daughter of Nikatau, a woman as capable as a man'. In fact her military gains were far greater than her father's, and she was as smart in defence as in attack.

- Vlad III surrounded his castle with a forest of spikes to impale traitors, invaders or perfectly innocent people to terrorize his enemies. Sometimes he arranged the spikes in geometric patterns to entertain himself.

- Lozen once left Victorio's band to rescue a mother with her new baby. First she braved gunfire to steal a horse from the Mexican cavalry for the mother to ride. She also stole a cowboy's horse and a soldier's rifle and ammunition for herself. Then she led the mother to safety.

- Genghis Khan used his siege machines to catapult hot boulders, bombs, and dead, decaying and diseased animals inside an enemy's stronghold. He hoped the carcasses would spread infection.

- Oda Nobunaga did not hesitate to murder his own family members. These included his Uncle Nobutomo and Uncle Shiba Yoshimune. With these two men out of the way, Nobunaga was able to take control of Owari province.

- Two foreign ambassadors visited Vlad III's court and refused to remove their hats politely in his presence. So Vlad ordered his guards to nail their hats to their heads.

GLOSSARY

BATTALION
A military unit

BLUDGEONING
Bashing

CAVALRY
Soldiers on horseback

COLONY
A nation ruled by an invading country

CORACLE
A small, circular, lightweight boat

DECOY
Something used to distract and confuse the enemy

FLANK
The right or left side of an armed unit

GUERRILLA
A tactic against a larger force using speed and stealth

IMPALE
To spike with a sharpened stake

INFANTRY
Foot soldiers

MACHETE
A long, flat, sharp-bladed cutlass

MAIM
To injure so that the victim cannot use their body well

MUSKET
A firearm loaded through the front end, or muzzle

PEZHETAIROI
Alexander the Great's column of foot soldiers bearing spears and shields

PIKEMAN
A soldier wielding any type of spear

PLUNDER
To take food, goods and treasure in an attack

RESERVATION
A fenced-in land in which a group of people are forced to live

SAHEL
A region in West Africa between the Sahara in the north and a forest region to the south

SARISSA
A long, sharp javelin or pike developed in Ancient Greece

SIEGE WEAPON
A huge, strong weapon that can batter defensive walls

31

INDEX

THE AUTHOR

Catherine Chambers was born in Adelaide, South Australia, grew up in the UK and studied African History and Swahili at the School of Oriental and African Studies in London. She has written about 130 books for children and young adults, and enjoys seeking out intriguing facts for her non-fiction titles, which cover history, cultures, faiths, biography, geography and the environment.

THE ILLUSTRATOR

Jason Juta is a South-African born illustrator living in London. He studied graphic design but turned to illustration, and works in two styles. He creates fantasy art digitally for the gaming industry (*Dungeons and Dragons* and *Star Wars*, for example), using 3D to work out perspective, and personal work based on photography, with dark, mythic themes, painted in a traditional way.

Picture Credits (abbreviations: t = top; b = bottom; c = centre; l = left; r = right)
© www.shutterstock.com: 6 tl, 6 bc, 7 cl
7 br Daniel Prudek / Shutterstock.com

CONTENTS

Words in **bold** can be found in the glossary on page 30.

Some of the projects in this book require scissors, paint and glue.
We would recommend that children are supervised by an adult
when using these things. One project also requires plaster of Paris. Children should
not be allowed to handle plaster of Paris and adults handling it should always wear gloves.

! The sea can be dangerous. Make sure you have
an adult with you when you visit the seaside.

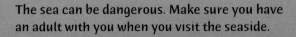

AT THE SEASIDE

The seaside is the border between the land and the ocean. All sorts of plants and animals live at the seaside, and of course people live there too.

The place where the land and the sea meet is called the seaside.

Scenery

Not all seaside scenery looks the same – there are lots of different types of coastline. There may be high cliffs, rocky **headlands** or sand **dunes**. You may find a beach covered with sand, pebbles or shells. Where a river meets the sea, there are often **mudflats**. All these places form **habitats** for different plants and animals.

QUIZ TIME!
Where else in the world do you think you might find sand dunes?

a. in a desert
b. in a forest
c. on a mountain

Answer on page 32.

Tides

Twice a day, the sea rises up the shore and then falls back again. These changes are called high **tides** and low tides. Tides are mainly caused by the pull of the Moon's **gravity** on the water. High and low tides happen at different times each day. An incoming tide can be dangerous because it can come in very quickly. If you go to the seaside, it's always good to know whether the sea is coming in or going out.

At high tide the beach is covered with water.

At low tide the water has gone and boats are left on the sandy beach.

Seaside records

The world's longest beach stretches for 240 kilometres along the coast of Brazil in South America. The Bay of Fundy in Canada has the biggest tides. The water rises and falls more than 11 metres here. The world's highest sea cliffs are on the islands of Hawaii, USA, in the Pacific Ocean.

Quick *FACTS*

- Different types of coasts are habitats for different plants and animals.
- Twice a day, tides rise and fall on the shore.

HAVE A GO

Find photos of the same beach at high and low tide. (If you are at the seaside, you can take your own photos.) Compare the two photos. What differences can you see?

ON THE BEACH

Beaches form in bays and inlets. A beach may be covered with sand, mud, pebbles, small stones or tiny shells.

! The sea can be dangerous, so make sure you have an adult with you. Never swim in the sea alone.

HAVE A GO
The next time you visit the seaside, take a walk from the upper shore (p. 7) down to the water's edge. Notice features in different zones, such as the high tide mark, **shingle**, sand, rocks and rockpools. Make a map of the beach. List or draw the plants and animals you see in the different zones.

Sea power

The scenery at the coast is shaped by the sea. Waves beat at the shore every minute of every day. This wears away the land in a process called **erosion**. Some rocks at the coast are softer than others and can wear away quickly, to form a wide bay or a narrow **inlet**. The sea drops sand, shells or other materials here to form a beach.

Some of the waves that crash onto coastlines can be huge!

Lower shore

Middle shore

Upper shore

The three main zones on a beach.

Worn by the waves

Most of the pebbles on a beach come from nearby rocks. As waves crash against the coast, bits of rock break off. As these pieces tumble in the waves, sharp corners and jagged edges are worn away to form smooth, rounded pebbles.

Beach zones

Rising and falling tides create zones on a beach. There are three main zones: the lower, middle and upper shores. The lower shore is covered with water, except when there is a very low tide. The upper shore is dry, except at high tide. The middle shore is covered with seawater at times; the rest of the time it is dry.

? What animals live in different zones on the beach? Turn the page to find out.

Seaweed left at the high tide mark on a beach.

Beach habitats

Each zone on the beach is home to its own set of plants and animals. Animals of the upper shore include small, shrimp-like sandhoppers, which lurk among seaweed that has been left at the high tide mark. Crabs hide in the sand and among rocks on the middle shore. Sea anemones (p. 15) and starfish live in rockpools on the lower shore.

A starfish clings to an underwater rock.

A rockpool on the lower shore.

QUIZ TIME!

Which of these animals might you find by the sea?

   a. cat
   b. dog whelk
   c. squirrel

Answer on page 32.

Quick FACTS

• Beaches form where pebbles, stones or sand build up in a bay or inlet.
• The upper, middle and lower shores are home to many different plants and animals.

Make this

Shells and other things you find on a beach are brilliant for craft projects. You could make a beach hut mirror to hang in your bathroom or bedroom.

You could use driftwood to make this into a photo frame instead. Or you could make a mirror that looks like a rockpool.

1 Cut a large rectangle of foam board as big as you want the finished hut to be. Glue strips of blue paper onto the foam board as shown.

2 Trim the sides and along the roof to make the shape of your beach hut.

3 Place a small rectangular mirror in the centre of your hut and draw around it. Ask an adult to carefully cut out the shape to make a rectangular hole.

4 Tape a piece of card over the hole on the back of your hut. Glue the mirror inside the hole and onto the card so the mirror side is facing out.

5 Glue sand and shells onto the foam board at the bottom of the beach hut. Tape a piece of string onto the back so you can hang up your mirror.

TIP: You can also buy shells from craft shops if you haven't visited a beach.

IN THE SAND

Sandy beaches are full of life, but most of it is hidden. Many animals live in burrows in the sand.

Wet sand has been made into a sandcastle on a beach.

What is sand?

Sand is made of tiny grains of rock and shell that have been smashed up by the waves and then dropped onto the shore. Just one square metre of beach contains millions of these grains. Sand is an amazing material. Dry sand runs through your fingers, but when it is wet, sand sticks together, so you can use it to build sandcastles.

Empty razor clam shells. Razor clams live in burrows in the sand.

A crab comes out of its sandy burrow. Crabs are scavengers – they eat anything they can find.

Crabs

You will often see crabs on a beach. Some types live in burrows in the sand. Others live in rockpools. Crabs have eight legs. They also have a pair of claws that can give you a nip if you're not careful. Crabs belong to a group of animals called **crustaceans**. This group includes shrimps and lobsters. They all have a hard body case or shell.

Buried in the sand

Two main groups of animals live in the sand: sea-snails, such as razor clams; and worms, such as ragworms and lugworms. Lugworms swallow sand and **filter** out tiny bits of food. Razor clams are also filter-feeders. Ragworms are **predators**. At high tide they come to the surface to look for **prey**, such as lugworms.

HAVE A GO
Lugworms live in U-shaped burrows. At the head end is a little pit, made by the worm as it swallows sand. The waste sand comes out its other end, to leave a little worm-shaped cast at the surface. Look for these lugworm casts on the beach.

TIP: If you can't visit a beach you can see similar casts in soil that have been made by earthworms.

? What leaves tracks in the sand?
? Turn the page to find out.

The collared plover is a type of shorebird.

Making tracks

Seabirds, crabs and other animals leave tracks on a sandy beach. Become a beach detective. Study the prints and try to identify the animals that made them. Each type of bird leaves different tracks. For example, gulls have **webbed** feet. Shorebirds such as turnstones have long, narrow toes. See if you can follow the tracks to find out where the animals went.

TIP: If you don't live by a beach you could follow tracks in mud that have been made by birds and animals in a wood or garden.

Shorebirds have left tracks in the sand with their feet.

Quick FACTS

- Sand is made of tiny grains of smashed up rock or shell.
- Many animals found on beaches live under the sand in burrows.

QUIZ TIME!

Most beaches have yellow or brown sand, but where can you find a beach with purple sand?

a. **Australia**

b. **Italy**

c. **the USA**

Answer on page 32.

Make this

Just like animal and bird tracks, shells and other objects pressed into sand leave marks too. You can make a paperweight by using sand to help you make a cast of a seashell.

! Plaster of Paris should only be handled by an adult.

You could make casts of other seaside objects, such as driftwood, for a seaside-themed display. Try painting them to look like real pieces of wood.

1 Fill a large plastic tub with sand. Mix it with water until the sand is damp, but not too wet.

2 Press the patterned side of some seashells firmly into the sand.

3 Gently remove the seashells. They should leave an impression in the sand. If the impression caves in when you take the shells out, your sand is either too wet or too dry. You will need to try again!

4 Ask an adult to mix up some plaster of Paris and carefully spoon the mixture into the impression in the sand. (Gloves must be worn when doing this and remember to wash the spoon!) Leave the mix to set. This will take a few days.

5 When the plaster has dried completely, lift out the shell shapes and brush off any sand. Paint the plaster shells with glue and cover them with glitter. Leave to dry.

IN A ROCKPOOL

Rockpools appear on rocky coasts when the tide has gone out. They are incredibly rich in wildlife, including small fish, shrimps, sea anemones and shellfish.

All change

Animals that live in rockpools have to cope with changing conditions. As the tide comes in, waves crash into the pool and swirling seawater fills it. At low tide the pool shrinks as the water drains back out. Rockpool creatures are specially **adapted** to survive in this changing environment.

At low tide this rockpool is partly filled with water.

Limpets have a very strong grip, which means they can cling onto seaside rocks.

Holding on!

Limpets and barnacles are shelled creatures that live in rockpools and on rocky shores. They cling onto rocks using the wide 'foot' on their underside. Their grip on the rock is very strong! At high tide, barnacles filter tiny bits of food from the water with their hairy legs.

 **HAVE A GO**

Have you ever tried to pick a limpet off a rock? They might seem to be stuck there, but in fact they move about to feed on tiny plants that grow on the rocks. Put a blob of model paint on some limpet shells. Make a map of their exact positions. Go back the next day to see if the limpets have moved. You could also use the same method to track garden snails.

Sea anemones

At low tide sea anemones look like blobs of jelly on the rocks. But at high tide they open up and spread their stinging **tentacles**. They look like plants but they are actually animals. Any small creatures that come within reach are captured by the tentacles and dragged into the sea anemone's mouth.

A sea anemone's mouth is surrounded by its stinging tentacles.

? What animals live in the shells you find on beaches? Turn the page to find out.

Winkles

Whelk

Topshell

Shells and shellfish

Shellfish are soft-bodied animals that live inside a hard shell. The main group are **molluscs**, which are related to garden snails.

Molluscs such as whelks, winkles and topshells have a single shell with a spiral shape. Scallops, cockles and mussels have two shells joined by a little hinge.

Scallop

Cockles

Mussels

Quick FACTS

- Rockpools are home to animals such as shrimps, starfish, molluscs and sea anemones.
- These creatures have to cope with changing conditions as tides rise and fall.

QUIZ TIME!

Which of these crabs is the smallest?

a. **blue crab**

b. **pea crab**

c. **spider crab**

Answer on page 32.

Make this

Seashells come in many different shapes and colours. You can create a seashell wind chime using the shells you find on a beach.

Shells come in many shapes and sizes because different animals live in them. What can you find out about the animals that lived in your wind chime shells?

TIP: You can also buy shells from craft shops if you haven't visited a beach.

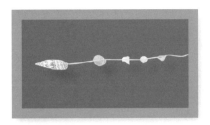

! You will need strong glue or a hot glue gun to do this - ask an adult to help you.

1
Cut four pieces of string, each piece about 30 cm long. It doesn't matter if they aren't exactly the same length. Place shells along each length of string. When you are happy with the layout, glue them in place.

2
When the glue has dried, tie one end of each string onto a twig.

3
Cut another length of string. Tie the ends of the string onto each end of the twig.

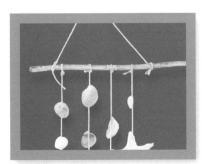

4
Hang the seashell wind chime in a breezy place, such as a window. The shells will clink together to create the wind chime effect.

IN THE WATER

Other wildlife, such as fish, seals and dolphins live in the sea. Seaweed also grows here.

This type of seaweed, which grows in deep water, is called kelp.

Seawater and seaweed

Seawater tastes salty because it is full of salt that has **dissolved** in it. Everything that lives in the sea is adapted to a saltwater habitat.

Seaweeds belong to a group of plants called algae. Many types can be found on the shore or in shallow water. Some types, such as kelp, grow in deep water. All seaweeds fix themselves to underwater rocks using a root-like part called a holdfast. They grow upwards towards the sunlight, which they need to make their food and grow.

Seals spend most of their time in the water, but sometimes come ashore.

Life underwater

Fish, crabs and starfish live among the seaweed. It is safer for them there as they can hide from predators. They also lay their eggs there to help keep them safe. Like all animals, they breathe **oxygen**, but they don't come to the surface to get it. Instead they **absorb** oxygen from the water using feathery structures called **gills**.

Marine mammals

Coastal waters are home to **mammals** such as seals and dolphins. Seals come ashore to **bask** on rocks in the sunshine and to have their young. Dolphins live in the water all of the time. They are naturally curious and sometimes follow boats. Like all mammals they cannot breathe underwater. They come to the surface of the water to breathe air.

QUIZ TIME!

Which of these animals can't breathe underwater?

a. octopus

b. whale

c. shark

Answer on page 32.

Smaller sea creatures, such as these kelp bass, feel safer swimming among the seaweed.

? Which fish hide on the seabed? Turn the page to find out.

Hiding on the seabed

If you stand in the shallows and look down, you may be lucky enough to spot a flatfish, such as a plaice. These flattened fish rest on the seabed. The colours and patterns on their bodies exactly match the seabed. This **camouflage** makes them very hard to find.

Beachcombers find all kinds of things on a beach, such as old fishing nets and shells.

HAVE A GO

Things from the sea can wash up on beaches. Items you find on the shore give clues about the plants and animals that live in the water. Become a **beachcomber**. Look for shells, egg cases and crab claws among the seaweed. You may find jellyfish, starfish and sea urchins washed up on the beach.

Quick FACTS

• Fish, starfish and seaweeds live in the waters off the coast.
• Flatfish, such as plaice, use camouflage to hide on the seabed.

Make this

Seaweed grows in beautiful shapes. Make seaweed pictures using a blown paint technique. You could use it to make a seaweed background for an underwater scene.

These blown paintings look brilliant grouped together in different colours. You can also use the same technique to create plants, such as trees and shrubs.

1 Water down some poster or watercolour paint so that it is runny. Dip the end of a straw into the paint and use the straw to 'draw' the basic shape of your seaweed.

2 Use the end of the straw to draw thinner branches sprouting from the main branches as shown. (You could use a picture of some seaweed to help you decide what shape your seaweed should be.)

3 Before the paint dries, gently blow the it through the other end of the straw. The paint on the paper will fan out and make lovely shapes that look like seaweed. Leave to dry.

ON THE CLIFFS

Cliffs form at the coast where hills made of hard rock edge the ocean. Cliffs provide homes for plants, insects, spiders and nesting birds.

The sea has worn a deep groove into these cliffs. There is now a beach where part of the cliff was.

Crumbling cliffs

Cliff coastlines are constantly changing as the edge of the land is worn away by the sea. As waves crash against the base of the cliffs, they wear a groove. The groove gets deeper and deeper, and finally the rocks on top collapse. Crumbling cliffs are dangerous, so never go too close to the edge.

QUIZ TIME!
Which of these birds like to nest on sea cliffs?

a. blackbirds
b. robins
c. terns

Answer on page 32.

Seaside plants

Clifftops are breezy places. They are home to plants that don't mind the salty air or the strong winds blowing off the ocean. These tough plants include gorse and heather. Thrift and campion grow close to the ground, out of the wind. Their flowers attract insects such as bees and butterflies, and also spiders that prey on insects.

Insects such as butterflies visit seaside flowers to drink nectar.

Puffins like to perch on steep cliffs. This helps the birds to keep away from any predators.

Nesting birds

Steep cliffs may be dangerous for people, but they are great places to rear your young if you can fly. Seabirds, such as puffins, nest in **colonies** on narrow ledges, where their eggs and young are safe from most predators. Puffins and gannets dive into the ocean to catch fish for their young.

? What is a seaside food chain? Turn the page to find out.

Gannet

Seaside food chains

Seaside animals eat plants or other animals. In turn, they may be eaten by larger predators. Diagrams called food chains show who eats what. Gannets feed on fish called mackerel, which feed on tiny shrimp-like crustaceans, such as **copepods**. The gannet, mackerel and shrimp form a simple food chain.

Mackerel

Mackerel

HAVE A GO
Seabirds, such as gannets, dive into the sea to catch fish like mackerel. Other birds fish from the surface. Use binoculars to spot seabirds fishing. Binoculars are also useful for watching birds anywhere.

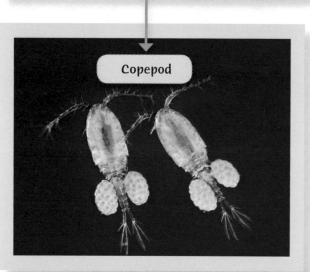

Copepod

Quick FACTS

- Cliffs form habitats for wildlife, such as plants, insects, spiders and seabirds.
- Wave erosion causes cliffs to crumble.
- Many seabirds live in colonies.

Make this

Food chain mobiles are a great way to show who eats what at the seaside. This mobile shows the food chain of a puffin, which hunts sand eels. Sand eels feed on smaller fish.

You can make food chains for animals that live in all kinds of habitats. Or you could make the puffin food chain longer by adding in what the small fish eat. Do you think puffins are eaten by any other animals?

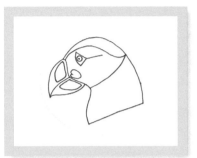

1 Draw a puffin on a piece of paper. You could trace this one or you can copy one from a book or from the Internet.

2 Cut out your puffin. Paint or colour it in and then glue it onto a circle of coloured card.

3 Cut out a few long sand eel shapes from silver foil. Glue them onto a circle of coloured card. Cut out lots of tiny fish shapes and glue them onto another circle of coloured card.

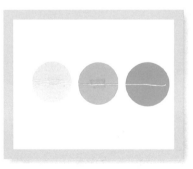

4 Lay your circles face down in a line. Make sure you get the order of your food chain right! Tape a length of string onto the back and tape a loop at the top to hang up your food chain.

LIVING AT THE SEASIDE

Coasts are popular places to live and go on holiday. People use the sea for food, minerals, energy and transport. About one in every five people in the world lives by the sea.

Food from the sea

The sea is an important source of food such as fish, crabs, shrimps and lobsters. Some types of seaweed are also eaten and seasalt is used to flavour food.

People have gathered food from the sea since **prehistoric** times. Seaside villages and towns often grow up around natural harbours that offer shelter for fishing boats.

Fishermen working on board their boat.

Minerals and energy

The sea is also a valuable source of **minerals**. Gold, silver and copper are mined from the seabed. A type of gem called a pearl forms inside the shells of a type of mollusc, called an oyster.

Oil and natural gases are sometimes drilled from the seabed of coastal waters. Seashores also help make energy. The power from wind, waves and tides can be used to make electricity.

Transport and trade

For hundreds of years the sea has been used as a highway, to move goods and people around the coast or across the sea to faraway places. Small fishing villages grew into ports, and then busy towns and cities that became centres for trade and industry. The sea is still the cheapest way of transporting goods between countries.

Giant cranes unload cargo from a ship at a busy port.

QUIZ TIME!

Pearls are found inside oysters, but what is inside a natural pearl?

a. a tiny animal

b. a grain of sand

c. nothing

Answer on page 32.

? Can you think of any other ways people use the seaside? Turn the page to find out.

Tourism

The seaside is a very popular place to go on holiday. About 60 years ago, cheap air travel arrived and people began to go abroad for their holidays. Now tourism is big business in many countries. Whether at home or abroad, the seaside is a great place to swim, relax and explore, or just enjoy the scenery. Coastlines all over the world are now popular **resorts**.

A beach at a resort in Palawn, Philippines.

Holiday-makers enjoy the sunshine, sand and sea at a beach in Romania.

Quick FACTS

- The seaside is a popular place to live and visit.
- The sea provides food, minerals, energy and a means of transport.
- Many people go to the seaside for their holidays.

HAVE A GO

Research a resort and make a list of what goes on there. Are boats in the harbour used for fishing, mining, trade or transport? Does tourism provide jobs for sailors, tour guides and people working in cafés, restaurants and shops? Make a poster showing what your resort has to offer.

Make this

Stencils are a great way of using simple patterns to build up a picture. You can make your own seaside themed cards and envelopes.

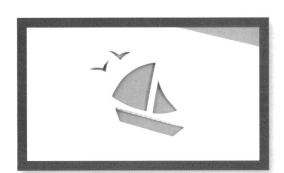

You can make all sorts of other amazing things using stencils. Simple starfish and shell shapes would make a funky design for wrapping paper, or some party invitations!

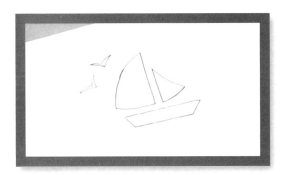

1 Draw a simple outline of a picture, such as a sailing boat and some seabirds.

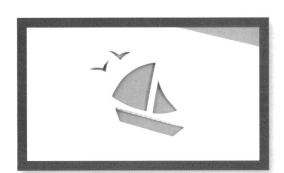

2 Ask an adult to cut out the middle of your design with a craft knife.

3 Tape the stencil onto whatever you want to decorate, such as a card and an envelope. Load your paintbrush with some paint and then dab off any excess on a scrap of paper. Dab the paint through the stencil. Remove the stencil and then leave the paint to dry.

4 You can repeat your design as many time as you like and you can also try using different colours, too.

GLOSSARY

absorb to take in

adapted suitable for something

bask to lie in the sun

beachcomber a person who looks for things on a beach

camouflage colours and patterns on an animal's body that help it blend in with its surroundings

colonies large groups of animals, such as seabirds, which live close together

copepods tiny shrimp-like crustaceans that are food for fish such as mackerel

crustaceans a group of (usually) marine animals with a hard body case

dissolves when a solid becomes part of a liquid

dunes mounds of sand

erosion when the land is worn away by natural forces, such as water

filter to remove small bits

gills the feathery parts on fish and other sea animals, which are used to absorb oxygen from the water

gravity the force that pulls one object towards another

habitat natural home of plants and animals

headlands rocky areas that jut out into the sea

inlet a bay or a narrow passage of water on the coast

mammals animals that have hair and feed their young on milk

mined dug from the ground

mineral a natural non-living substance

mollusc a type of animal with a soft body, such as a slug, a snail or a limpet

mudflats muddy banks, often at the mouth of a river (where the river meets the sea)

oxygen gas in the air that living things need to breathe

predators animals that hunt other animals for food

prehistoric the time before written records were made

prey animals that are hunted for food

resorts holiday towns or villages, which are often at the seaside

shingle small stones on a beach

tentacles long feelers, often covered with stinging needles. Used by sea creatures to capture their food

tides the rise and fall in sea levels on the coast

webbed the skin between an animal's toes, which make its feet work like paddles

BOOKS

Geographywise: Coasts
by Jen Green (Wayland Books, 2012)

History Snapshots: The Seaside
by Sarah Ridley (Franklin Watts, 2011)

Nature Trail: Seaside
By Jen Green (Wayland Books, 2010)

A Walk From: Our Seaside School
by Deborah Chancellor
(Franklin Watts, 2014)

WEBSITES

www.activityvillage.co.uk/seaside
Puzzles, crafts, colouring pages and
activities that are all about the seaside.

www.kids.nationalgeographic.com/kids/
Find out about some seaside animals, such
as starfish and puffins, or have fun with
the rockpool puzzles.

**http://studyjams.scholastic.com/
studyjams/jams/science/index.htm**
On this site find out about all kinds of
things relating to the seaside, such as
waves, erosion, tides and the animals
that live there.

**NOTE TO PARENTS
AND TEACHERS:**
Every effort has been made
by the Publishers to ensure
that these websites are
suitable for children, that
they are of the highest
educational value, and
that they contain no
inappropriate or offensive
material. However, because
of the nature of the Internet,
it is impossible to guarantee
that the contents of these
sites will not be altered. We
strongly advise that Internet
access is supervised by a
responsible adult.

INDEX

QUIZ ANSWERS

Page 4: a – in a desert. The biggest sand dunes in the world are in the Sahara desert in Africa.

Page 8: b – a dog whelk

Page 12: c – in the USA (Pfeiffer Beach, California)

Page 16: b – pea crab

Page 19: b – a whale

Page 22: c – terns

Page 27: a – a tiny animal (which gets trapped inside an oyster's shell)